Scroll Saw Holiday Patterns

Patrick and Patricia Spielman

 Sterling Publishing Co., Inc.   New York

Library of Congress Cataloging-in-Publication Data

Spielman, Patrick E.
    Scroll saw holiday patterns/by Patrick & Patricia Spielman.
        p.   cm.
    Includes index.
    ISBN 0-8069-8476-7 (pbk.)
    1. Jig saws. 2. Woodwork. 3. Holiday decorations. I. Spielman,
Patricia. II. Title.
TT186.S6733 1991
684′.083—dc20   91-21981
                                                                          CIP

Edited by Rodman Neumann

10   9   8   7

© 1991 by Patrick & Patricia Spielman
Published by Sterling Publishing Company, Inc.
387 Park Avenue South, New York, N.Y. 10016
Distributed in Canada by Sterling Publishing
% Canadian Manda Group, P.O. Box 920, Station U
Toronto, Ontario, Canada M8Z 5P9
Distributed in Great Britain and Europe by Cassell PLC
Villiers House, 41/47 Strand, London WC2N 5JE, England
Distributed in Australia by Capricorn Ltd.
P.O. Box 665, Lane Cove, NSW 2066
Manufactured in the United States of America
All rights reserved

Sterling ISBN 0-8069-8476-7

Contents

Color section follows p. 64

About the Authors

Patrick Spielman's love of wood began when, as a child, he transformed fruit crates into toys. Now this prolific and innovative woodworker is respected worldwide as a teacher and author.

His most famous contribution to the woodworking field has been his perfection of a method to season green wood with polyethylene glycol 1000 (PEG). He went on to invent, manufacture, and distribute the PEG-Thermovat chemical seasoning system.

During his many years as shop instructor in Wisconsin, Mr. Spielman published manuals, teaching guides, and more than 30 popular books, including *Modern Wood Technology*, a college text. He also wrote six educational series on wood technology, tool use, processing techniques, design, and wood-product planning.

Author of the best-selling *Router Handbook*, Mr. Spielman has served as editorial consultant to a professional magazine and as advisor and consultant to power tool manufacturers, and his products, techniques, and many books have been featured in numerous periodicals and on national television.

This pioneer of new ideas and inventor of countless jigs, fixtures, and designs used throughout the world is a unique combination of expert woodworker and brilliant teacher—all of which have endeared him to his many readers and to his publisher.

Patricia Spielman (Mrs. Pat) has co-authored three other books with her husband, Patrick, including their first and best-selling *Scroll Saw Pattern Book*. She is currently at work on a new book of Christmas patterns with Patrick and their daughter, Sandra. As both a buyer of wood products and the creator of Spielmans WoodWorks Gift Shop and Gallery, Mrs. Pat plays an invaluable role in the overall operations of the varied and well-known Spielmans WoodWorks businesses. Recently Mrs. Pat and daughter, Sherri Valitchka, opened a new gift gallery, Spielmans Kid Works, which features high-quality wood toys and furniture. Mrs. Pat is highly respected locally and nationally for her discerning eye for design and her natural artistic abilities, all of which are evident not only in the Spielmans' books, but also in their trend-setting WoodWorks Gallery.

Should you wish to contact the Spielmans, please send your correspondence to Sterling Publishing Company.

Acknowledgments

We thank our daughters, Sherri and Sandy, for their help. The shading on many of the designs making them better and more interesting patterns is the result of Sherri's efforts. And thanks to Sandy for assistance in painting many of the colorful cutouts.

A hearty thank-you to Dirk Boelman of The Art Factory for the finished art and for helping us complete everything in a timely manner.

Many thanks again to Julie Kiehnau, our expert scroll-sawyer and typist, for her outstanding work in both areas.

Patrick & Patricia Spielman
Spielmans Wood Works

Metric Conversion

Inches to Millimetres and Centimetres

MM—millimetres   CM—centimetres

Inches	MM	CM	Inches	CM	Inches	CM
⅛	3	0.3	9	22.9	30	76.2
¼	6	0.6	10	25.4	31	78.7
⅜	10	1.0	11	27.9	32	81.3
½	13	1.3	12	30.5	33	83.8
⅝	16	1.6	13	33.0	34	86.4
¾	19	1.9	14	35.6	35	88.9
⅞	22	2.2	15	38.1	36	91.4
1	25	2.5	16	40.6	37	94.0
1¼	32	3.2	17	43.2	38	96.5
1½	38	3.8	18	45.7	39	99.1
1¾	44	4.4	19	48.3	40	101.6
2	51	5.1	20	50.8	41	104.1
2½	64	6.4	21	53.3	42	106.7
3	76	7.6	22	55.9	43	109.2
3½	89	8.9	23	58.4	44	111.8
4	102	10.2	24	61.0	45	114.3
4½	114	11.4	25	63.5	46	116.8
5	127	12.7	26	66.0	47	119.4
6	152	15.2	27	68.6	48	121.9
7	178	17.8	28	71.1	49	124.5
8	203	20.3	29	73.7	50	127.0

Introduction

Scroll Saw Holiday Patterns contains over 300 new, individual designs and projects in nine major categories, providing ready-to-use patterns for most holidays and special family occasions. Most of these patterns are presented in what we think are usable full sizes. However, because individual needs and preferences vary, we hope that you will change the sizes of our patterns or modify them to satisfy your particular needs. For example, small hanging ornaments may be enlarged to make huge lawn-size or yard-size decorations, and conversely some of our larger cutouts can be reduced to make small hanging ornaments. Experiment with several changes of size, as desired.

Sizing, Copying and Transferring Patterns

The easiest and fastest way to enlarge or reduce patterns is with the assistance of a modern office copier machine. If one is not available for your use, there are other methods you can use that have traditionally been used for enlarging drawings, such as using square grids or pantographs.

A copier-machine-enlarged pattern is highly desirable, because it is accurate and it can be applied directly to the wood for the sawing guide (Illus. 1). The copies can be temporarily bonded directly onto the surface of the workpiece using a brush-on rubber cement or a *temporary* bonding spray adhesive (Illus. 2). We prefer the spray-adhesive technique. There are several spray adhesives available that will work, but we recommend a spray mount artist's adhesive such as 3M's Scotch brand. Most photography stores and studios carry this, as do art graphics and craft supply stores. One can will last about a year. It's a great time-saving product.

To use the adhesive, simply spray a very light mist onto the back of the pattern copy—*do not spray on wood*—see Illus. 2. Wait 10 to 30 seconds, press the pattern copy onto your wood (Illus. 3) with hand pressure, and, presto! you're ready to begin sawing—just that easy and just that quick! Gone are the frustrations of doing tracings, working with messy carbon papers, and

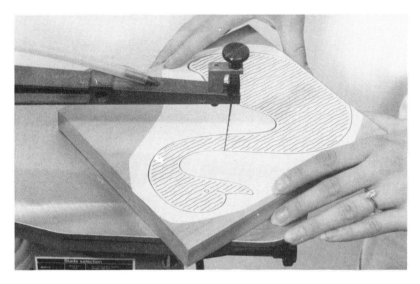

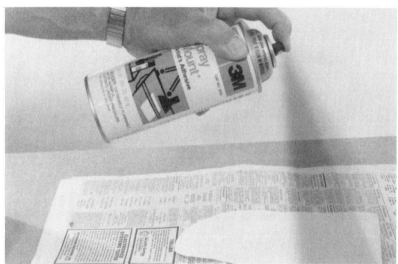

Illus. 1 Any small scroll saw can be used to make most of the projects in this book. Here one-inch-thick wood with a copied pattern applied to it is cut with a narrow blade.

Illus. 2 Apply a very light "mist" of spray adhesive only to the back of the pattern. Do not spray directly onto the wood. Note that a newspaper underneath the pattern is being used to catch the overspray.

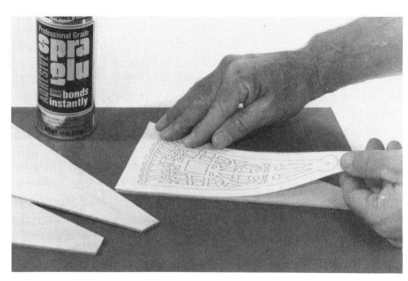

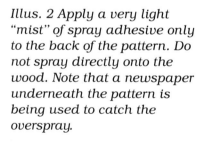

Illus. 3 Pressing down a spray-adhesive-coated copy of the pattern directly onto the wood workpiece blank.

similar techniques that never really produced the clear, crisp, accurate layout lines which are so essential to good sawing.

Saw following the same lines of the pattern. When sawing is completed, the pattern is easily peeled off the workpiece (Illus. 4). The adhesive virtually leaves no residue on the wood that might inhibit subsequent finishing. We also recommend that you test the tack qualities of the adhesive to be sure that, at first use, you are spraying just enough for an effective temporary bond, and no more.

If you decide to use the rubber-cement method to bond a machine-copied pattern to the workpiece, a little more care is required. Do not brush on too heavy a coat. If some cement remains on the wood after peeling off the pattern, it can be removed by rubbing it off with your fingers. *Do not use solvents!*

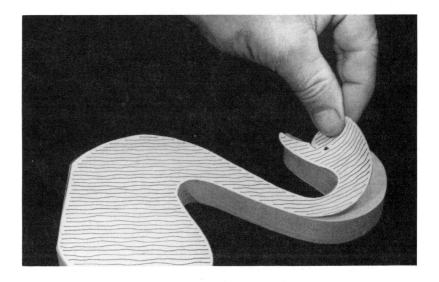

Illus. 4 After sawing is completed, the pattern lifts off the wood easily, leaving no residue to interfere with finishing.

Stack-Sawing Techniques

Stack-sawing involves layering one or more pieces of wood on top of another and sawing them all at once. This technique produces perfectly identical cut pieces and saves time. The layers can be held together in a variety of ways, such as nailing or gluing in the waste areas, using double-faced tape (use very little), wrapping around the stack with masking tape, or stapling the layers together through the waste along the edges. All of the previous ways will work, and certain patterns are better handled with one method than another.

Tip: Use the spray adhesive applied to both sides of strips of paper to make your own double-faced tape. This trick works especially well when stack-sawing thin wood—wood too thin to nail or tack together.

Wood Materials

These patterns can be made from a wide variety of different materials and in a variety of different thicknesses—most of these choices are entirely yours. In some cases we specify or suggest suitable thicknesses where it's important to the visual impact or

9

structural requirements of a particular design. Use cheap soft woods, as a practical choice, if the cutouts are to be coated with opaque finishes. Some of the more highly detailed fretted designs may be best sawn from plywoods that are more durable but sometimes less attractive than solid woods.

Ways to Utilize Patterns

In addition to enlarging or reducing patterns to your own size preferences, there are several other ways to individualize patterns. Wall-hanging designs can be made into utility projects by adding pegs or hooks to hang various things on. Standing designs can be converted to door stops simply by nailing a thin wedge to the back side. Glue on magnets to make refrigerator-type note holders. Use designs as overlay decorations on boxes, clocks, signs, furniture, and various household accessories. Hang ornaments and/or stand cutouts in windows. Attach metal findings to the backs of minicutouts with epoxy glue to make jewelry. Add glued-on bows, lace, and pieces of fabric to give personality and color to otherwise bland cutouts.

Finishing Cutouts

There are lots of ways and different materials to finish your holiday cutout decorations and ornaments (Illus. 5). Natural finishes, stains, and paints are all good, with your choice a matter of personal preference. Many patterns have lines on the "face" of cutouts to give them some personality or character. Lines representing eyes, mouth, clothes, and the like can be painted (Illus. 6) or wood-burned (Illus. 7)—whatever is in line with your artistic inclinations.

Some patterns lend themselves well to *segmentation*. This is where lines of the pattern that suggest certain expressive features are cut apart (into segments). All sawn edges are rounded slightly using sandpaper pads (Illus. 8), or files (Illus. 9).

The individual pieces (segments) are put

Illus. 5 One pattern made in three different ways. Left to right: wood-burned line detailing, painted, and segmented, in which each individual part is cut free, stained (or painted) a different color and reassembled (glued) together to make the object whole again.

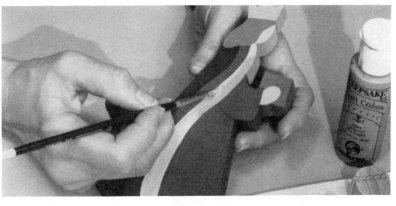

Illus. 6 Use colorful paints for pattern details.

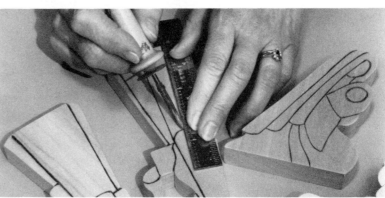

Illus. 7 Wood-burning pattern line details. Using a metal straightedge guide may be helpful.

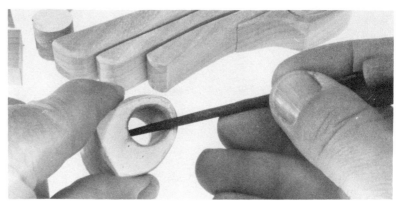

Illus. 8 Slightly rounding over the sawn edges of all segmented pieces. Here a folded piece of 60- or 80-grit abrasive sandpaper is flexed to match and sand an inside curved edge.

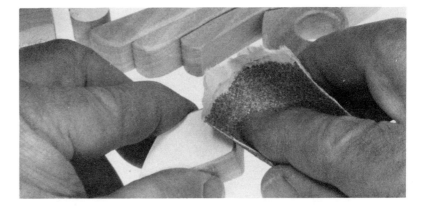

Illus. 9 Use a small file to round edges in tight areas.

back together again (Illus. 10) prior to being stained or painted (Illus. 11). Glue the segments to each other to make the whole.

If scroll sawing is new for you, we recommend *Scroll Saw Basics* (see page 157). This book provides essential instruction on scroll saws and on how to use them to make basic cuts.

Illus. 10 Checking the sanded edges of this segmented project with a trial assembly.

Illus. 11 Segmentation can also incorporate the combination of natural, stained, and painted pieces as desired. Leave inside gluing edges unfinished.

Patterns

18

Decorative Valentine "thought" sawn from thin plywood and painted red and white.

Cutouts in one-inch natural soft maple accented with red painted hearts.

Heart made from ½"-thick plywood with a ¼"-thick plywood overlay.

Be My Valentine

21

24

Simple heart cutouts can be enhanced by any combination of silk flowers, ribbon, or lace, glued-on with hot-melt adhesive.

Heart cutouts made from ⅝″ to ¾″ solid wood with rounded edges and lace glued to back. Heart design, above right, is cut from ¼″ plywood.

26

Ornaments can be sawn from any stock from ⅛″ to ½″ thick.

28

A standing shamrock for St. Pat's Day is sawn from any material at least ¾" thick.

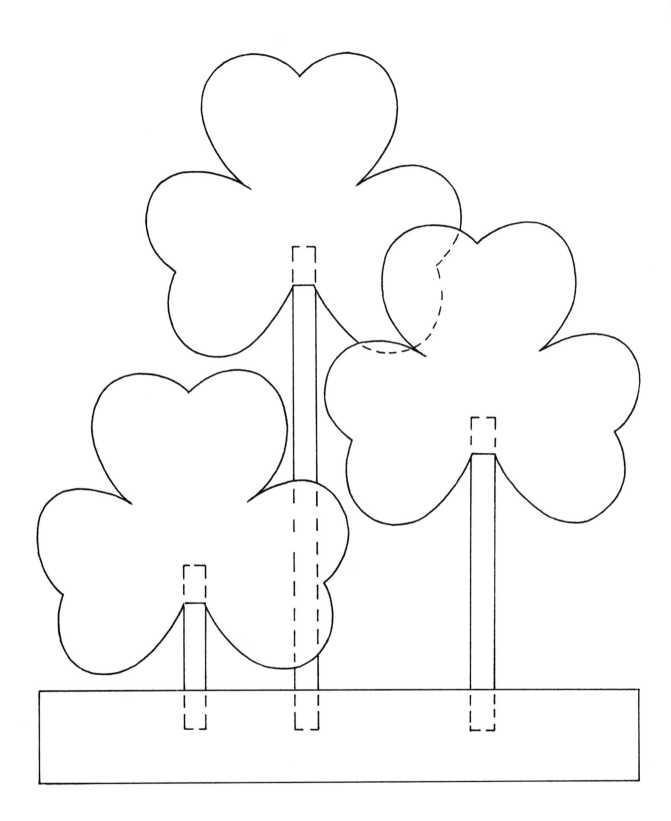

32

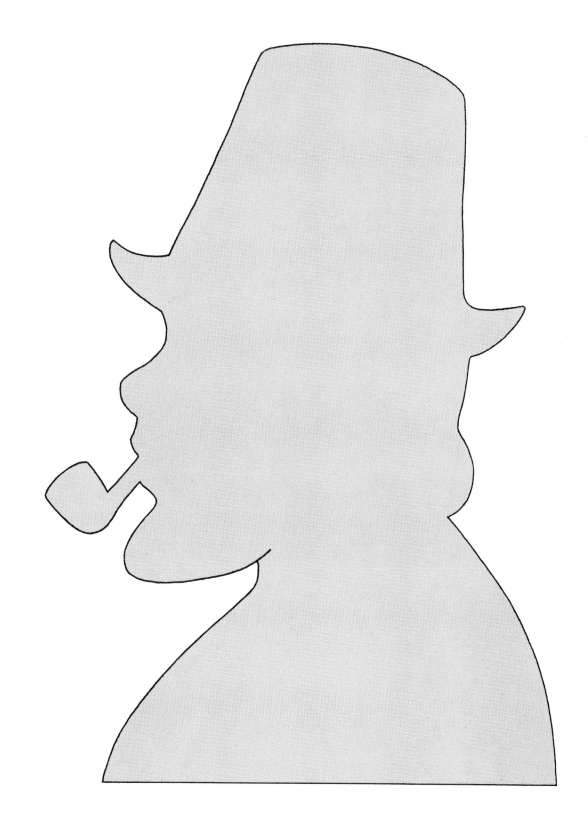

34

35

36

37

Standing bunny on the left has colorful pants of fabric applied with glue along with other painted details. Bunny on the right combines fretwork and painted detailing.

Easter design in ¾"-thick unfinished poplar.

Rocking bunny sawn from ¾"-thick and ½"-thick material decorated with paint, ribbon, and glued-on cotton tail.

41

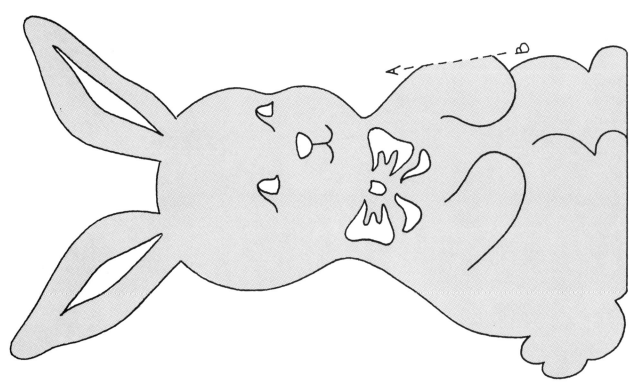

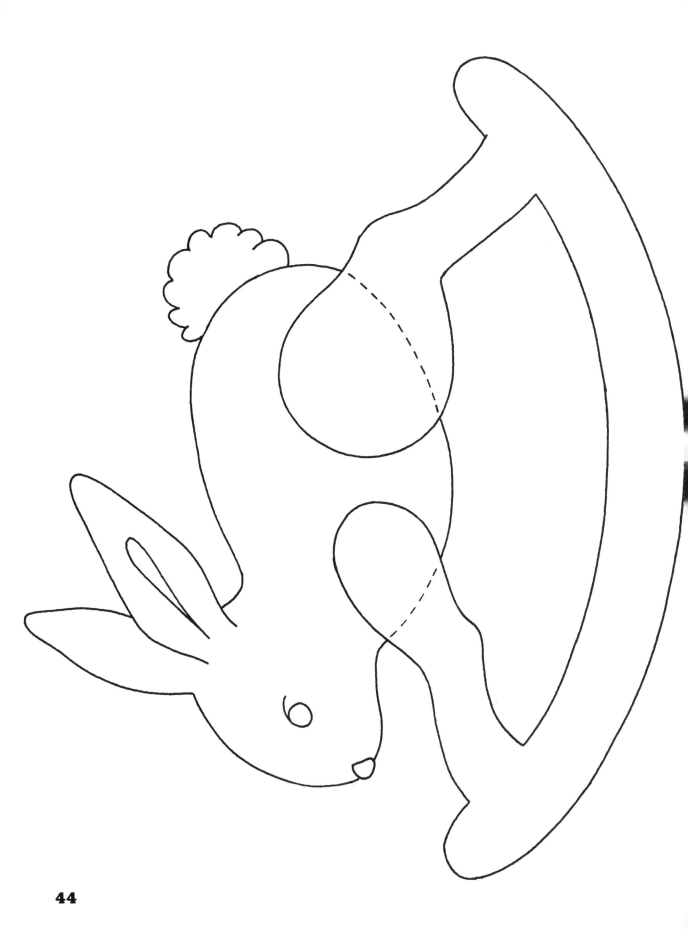

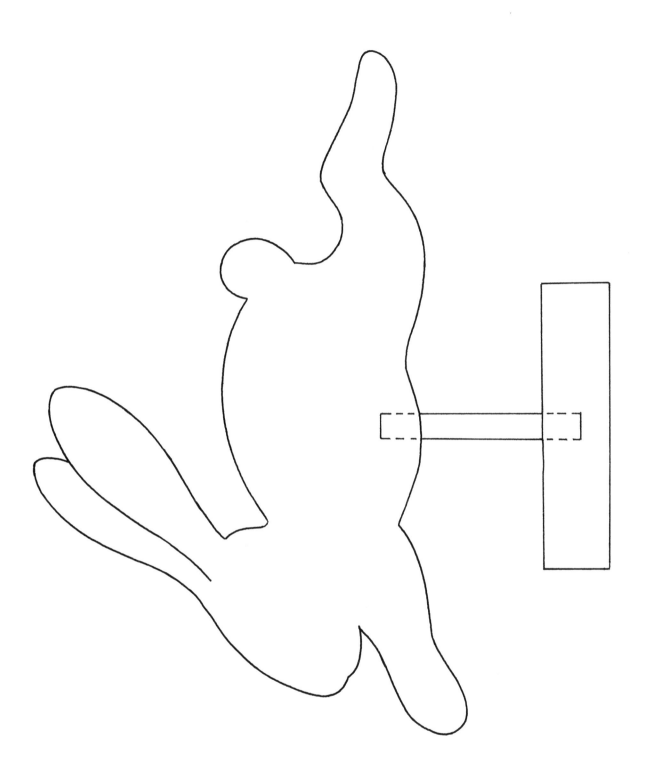

45

Dimensional bunnies made from ¾"-thick and ½"-thick material. Note the colorful ribbon used for the final decorative touch.

47

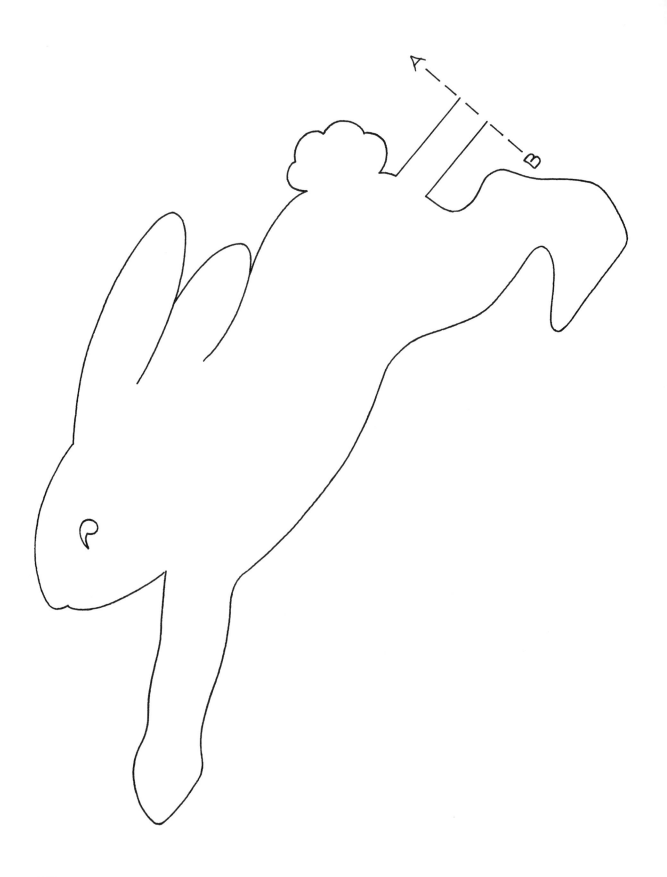

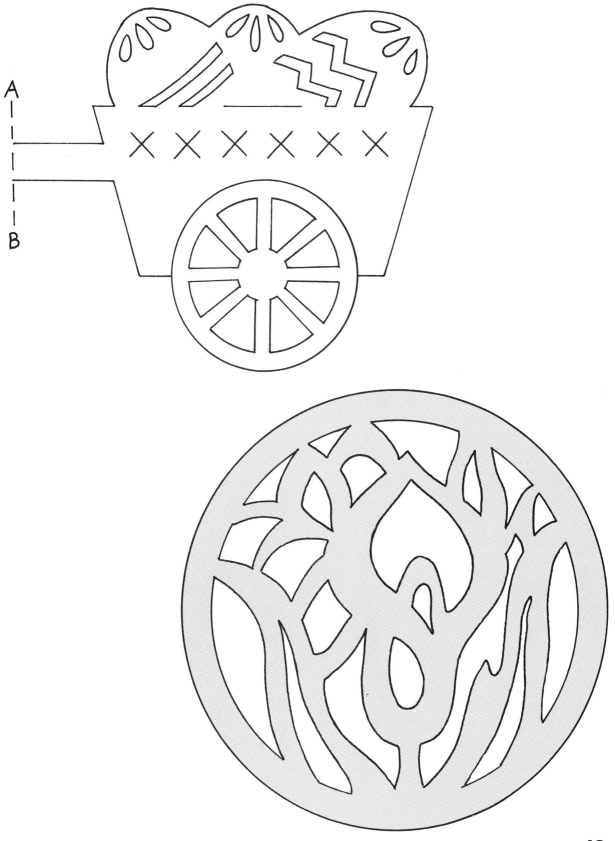

A

B

51

52

53

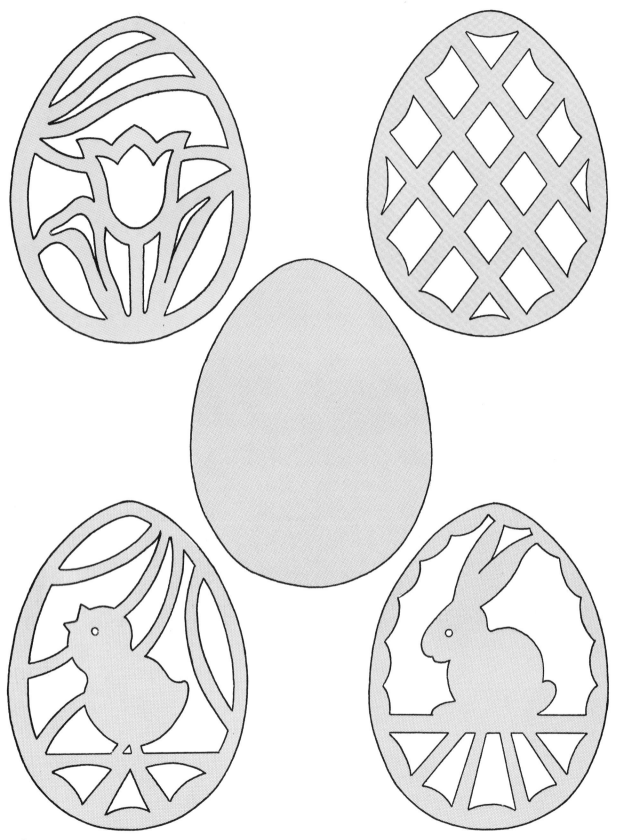

SHELF

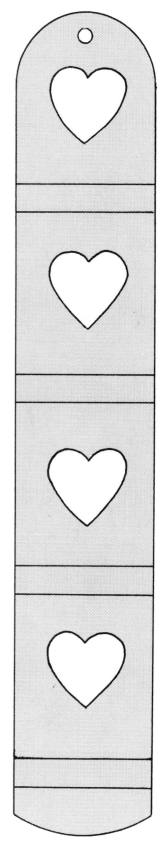

59

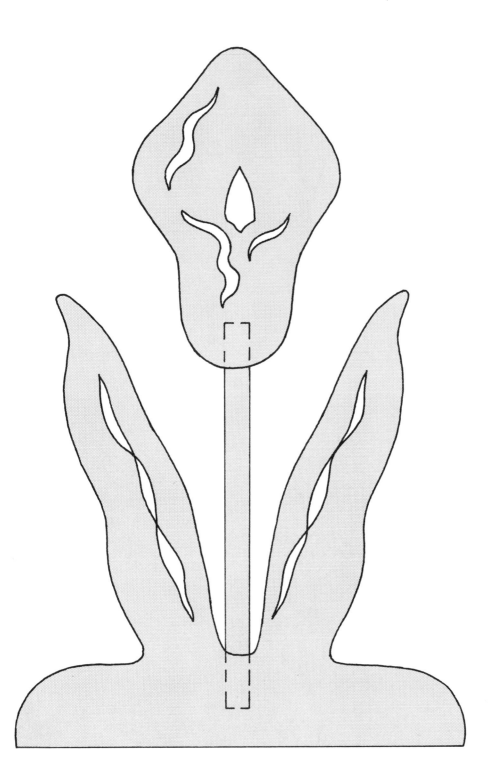

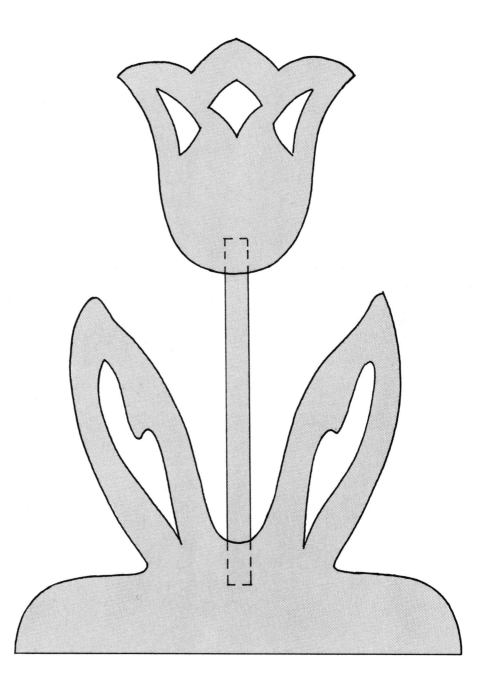

Easter egg cutout sawn from mahogany,
¾" thick.

Fretted Easter design cut from ¾"-thick mahogany.

63

A family of ghosts and other fun cutouts for Halloween.

A variety of Christmas fretwork sawn from birch plywood, left unfinished.

Painted cutouts, ¾"- to 1½"-thick material can be used.

A group of painted Christmas decorations.

B

Painted nativity set.

Nativity set characters made by the segmenting technique, with oil-stained colorization.

A variety of delicate, fretted ornaments made from thin domestic and exotic woods.

Wall hanging and standing Christmas decorations. The two at the right can also be used as trivets.

A variety of delicate, fretted ornaments made from thin domestic and exotic wood.

D

Fretwork Easter decorations sawn from ¾" mahogany, with natural oil finish.

A variety of delicate, fretted ornaments made from thin domestic and exotic woods.

Fretwork Easter decorations sawn from ¾" mahogany, with natural oil finish.

E

Make these painted ornaments from material ¼″ or less in thickness.

A shamrock among cutouts for Valentine's Day.

Variety of projects made from ¾"- and ½"-thick wood, painted, with ribbon and cotton used for interesting finishing touches.

Colorful Thanksgiving cutouts.

Christmas decorations made of ¾"-thick painted wood. Dimensional trees sawn from ¼"-thick material.

G

An ornament tree for any holiday, with interchangeable treetop designs.

These cutouts, a fretted pumpkin and solid cat, make an interesting combination.

Easter cutouts. Note the use of colorful fabric glued on as a decorating detail on the rabbit on the left.

H

65

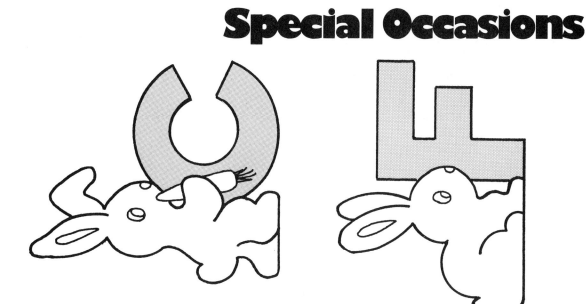

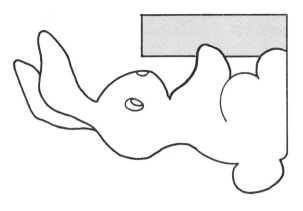

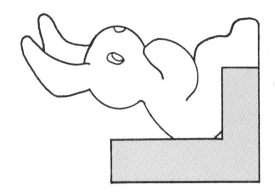

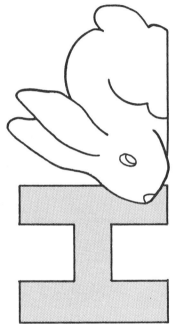

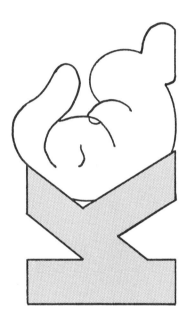

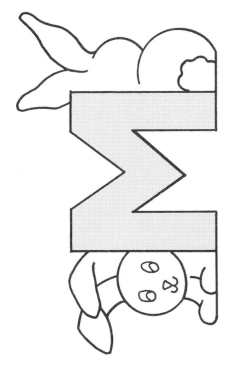

71

73

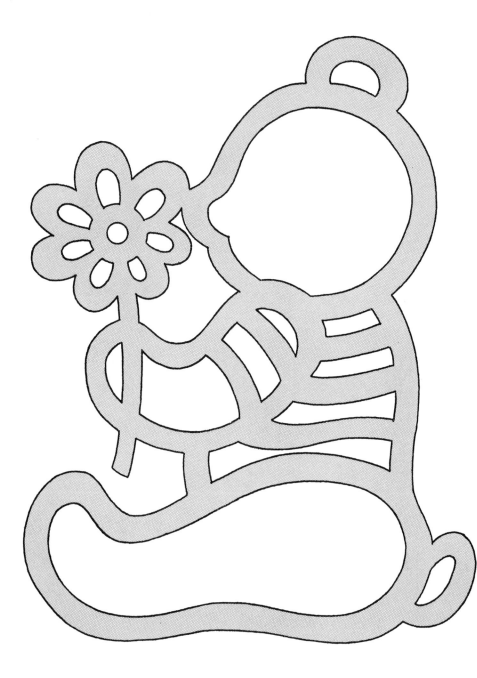

Patriotic Holidays

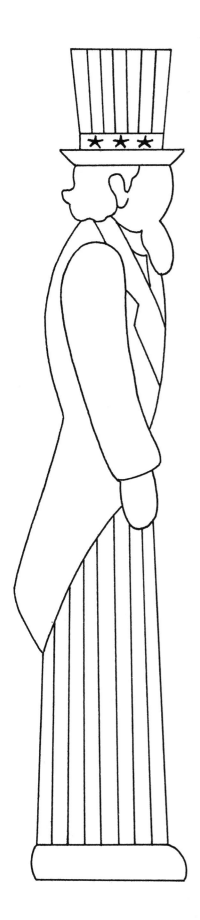
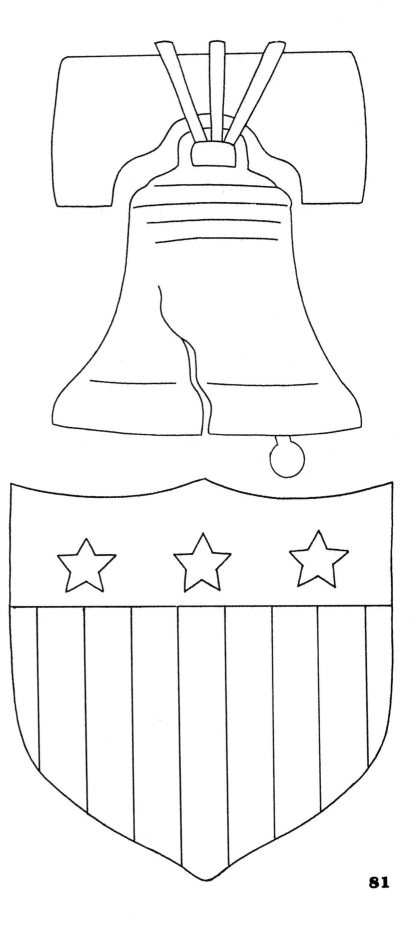

81

82

83

84

85

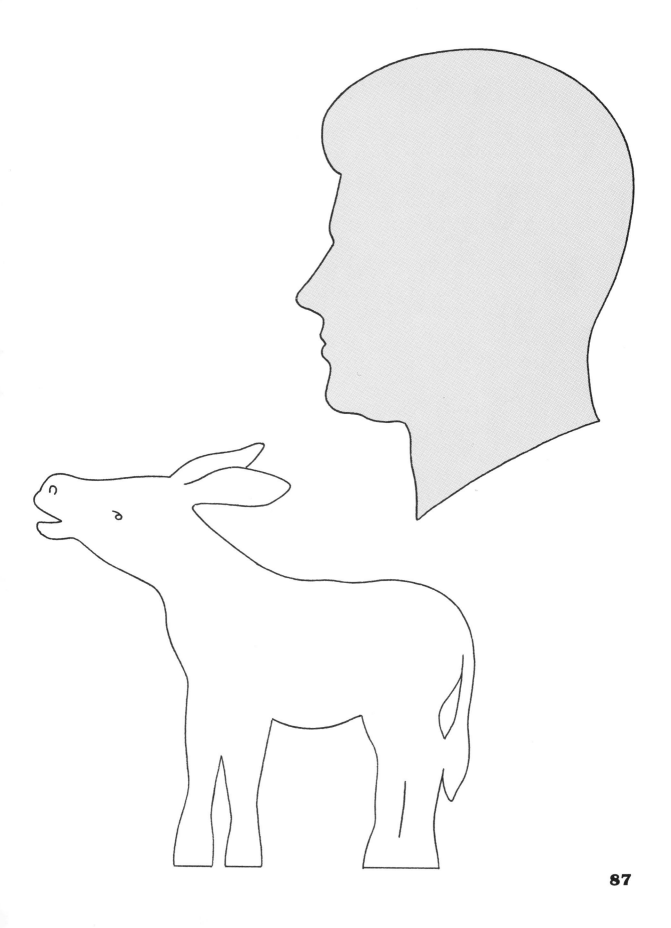

Halloween

Painted pine cutouts.

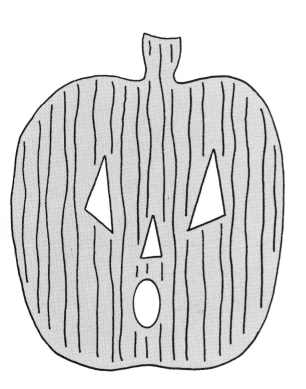

91

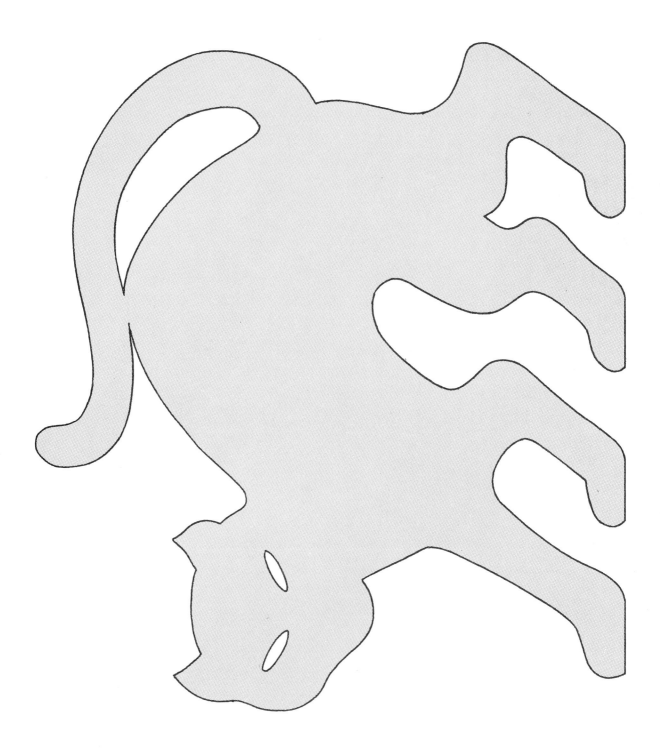

93

95

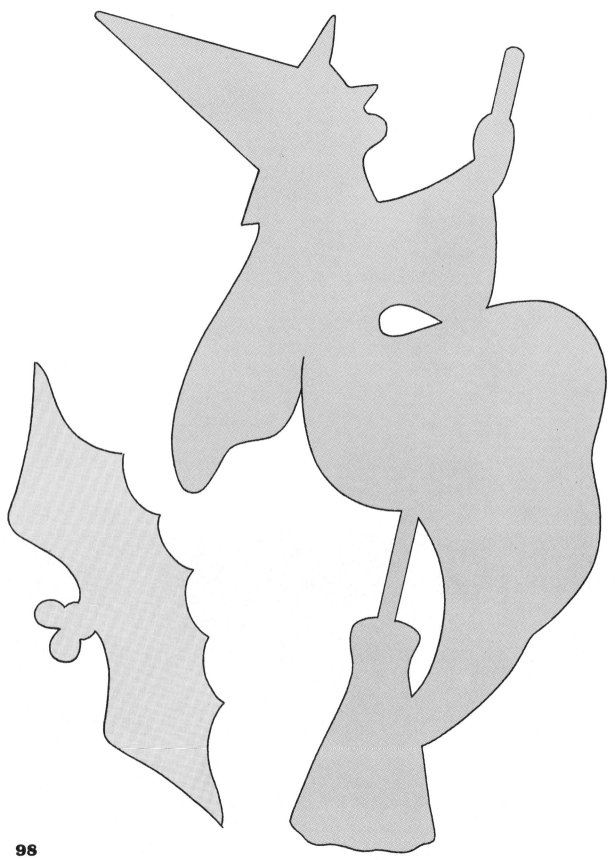

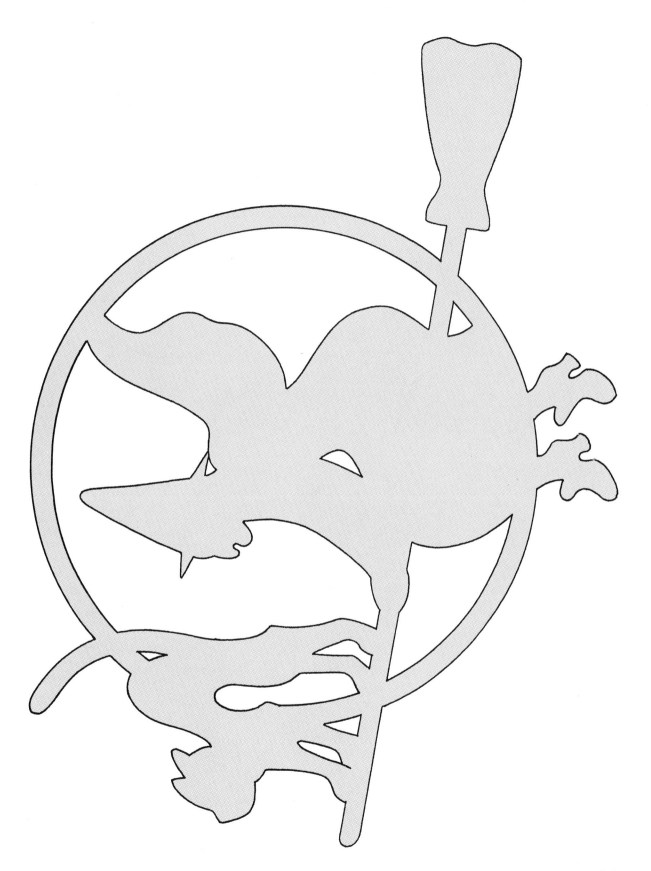

99

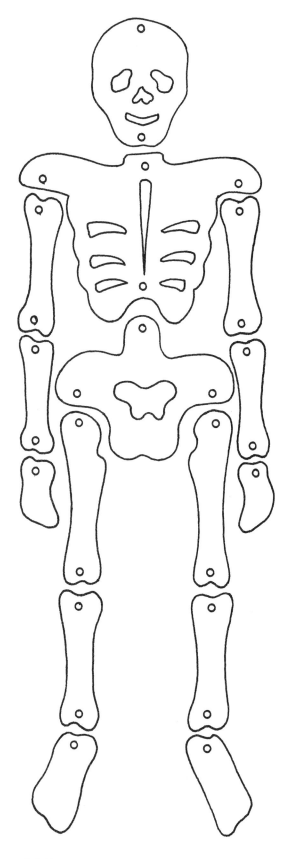

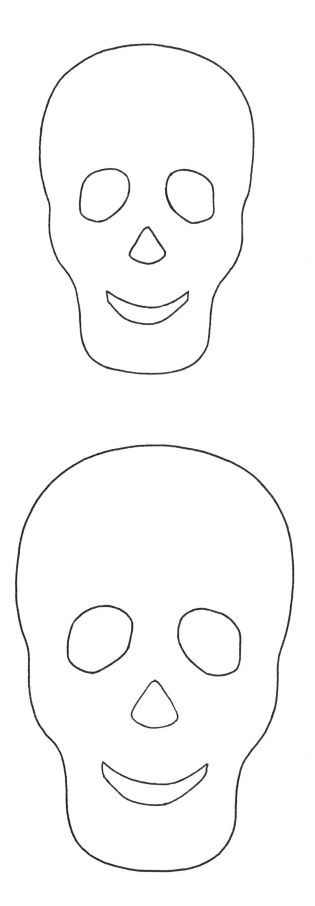

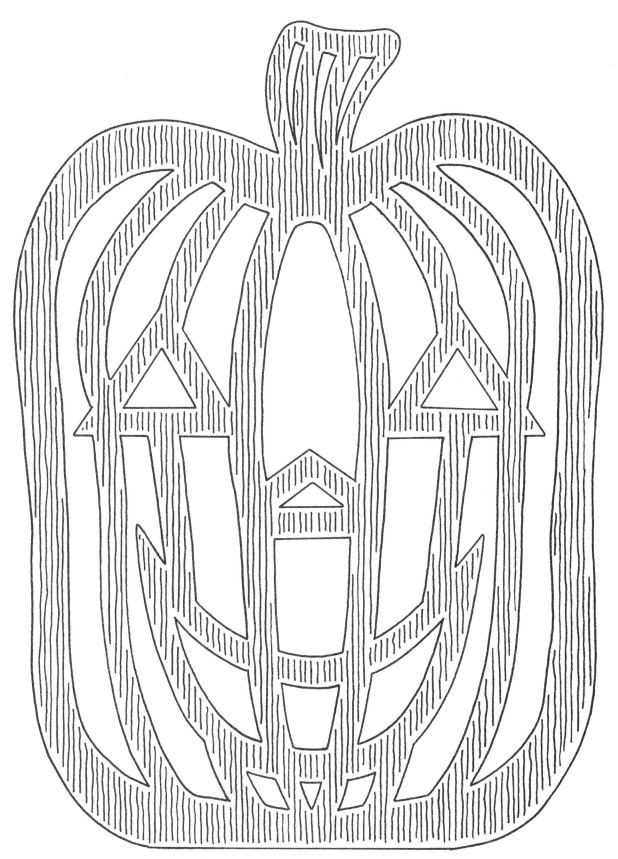

Thanksgiving

Thanksgiving cutouts made from ¾"-thick painted softwood with ½"-thick material used for the turkey wings.

107

Christmas

Segmented characters for the Nativity set.

Painted Nativity set.

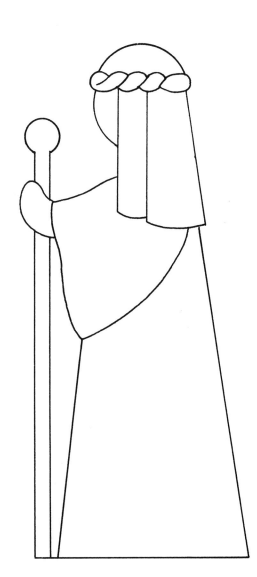

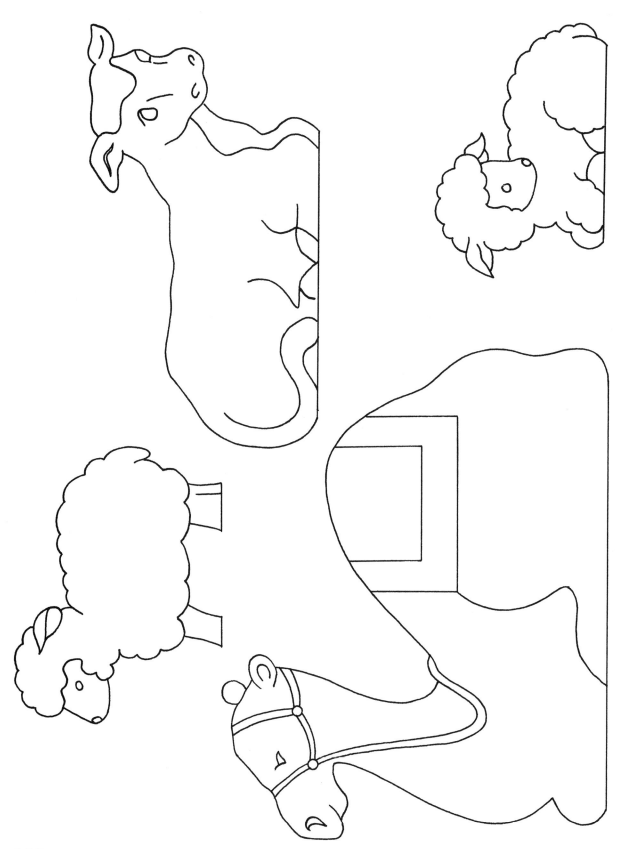

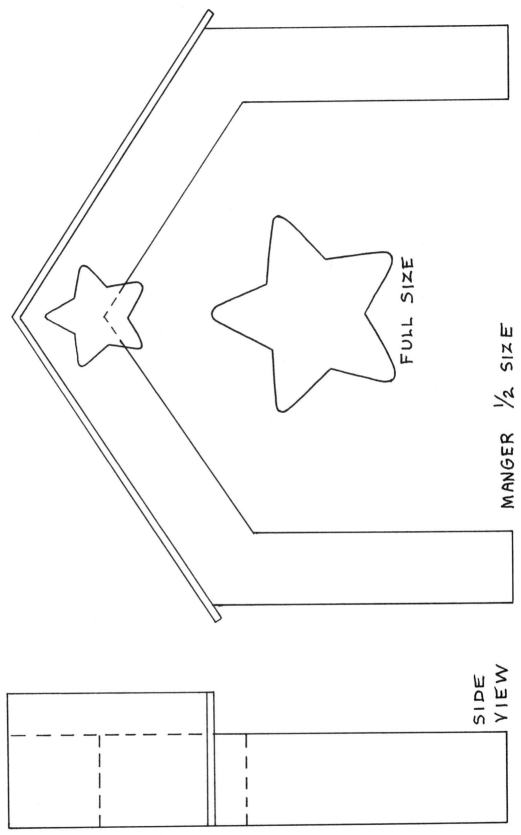

FULL SIZE

MANGER ½ SIZE

SIDE
VIEW

114

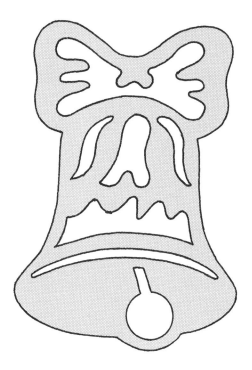

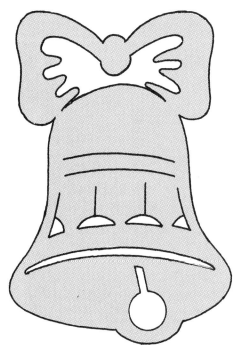

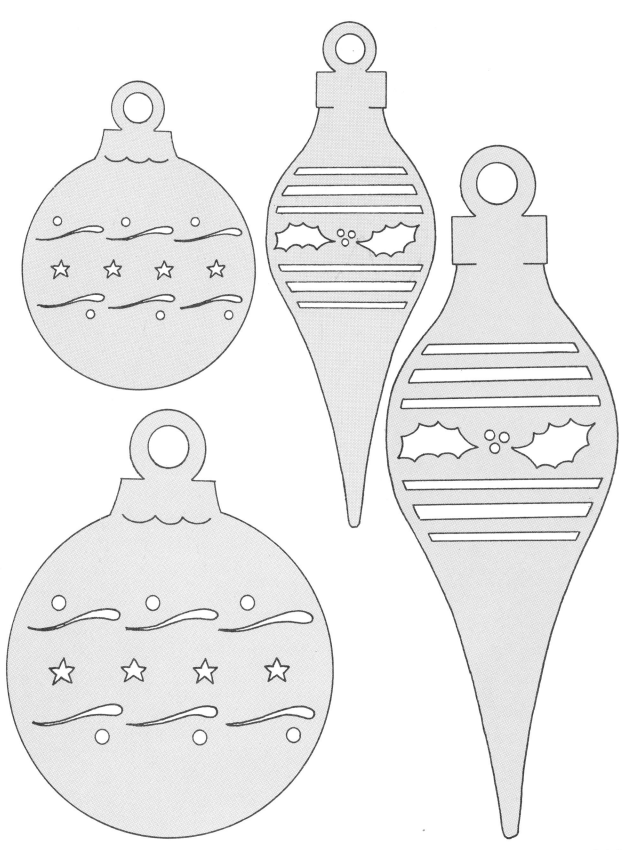

120

Snowman family cut from ¾"-
thick material and painted.

Mr. and Mrs. Santa sawn from
¾"-thick material and
painted.

Pair of Santas sawn from ¾"-
thick material.

121

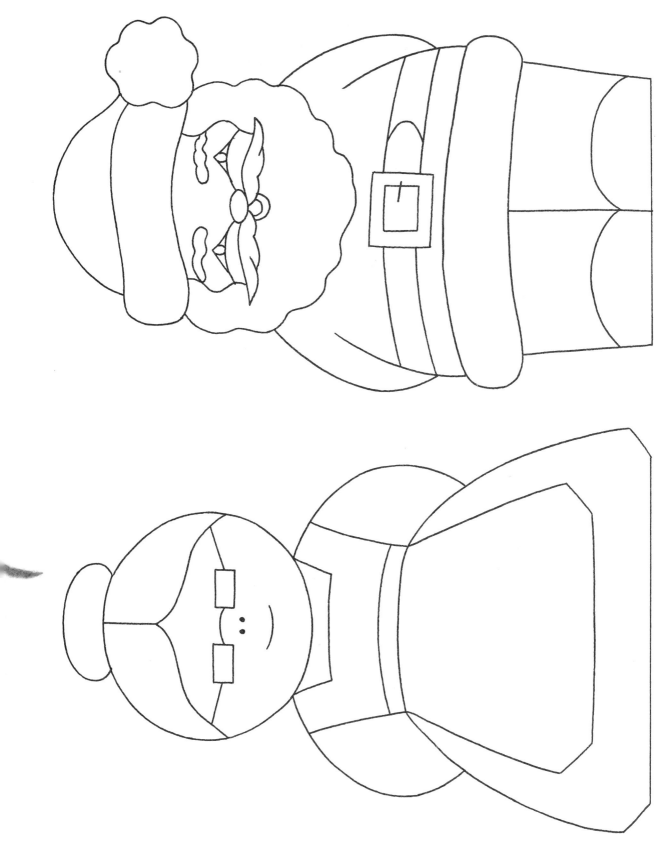

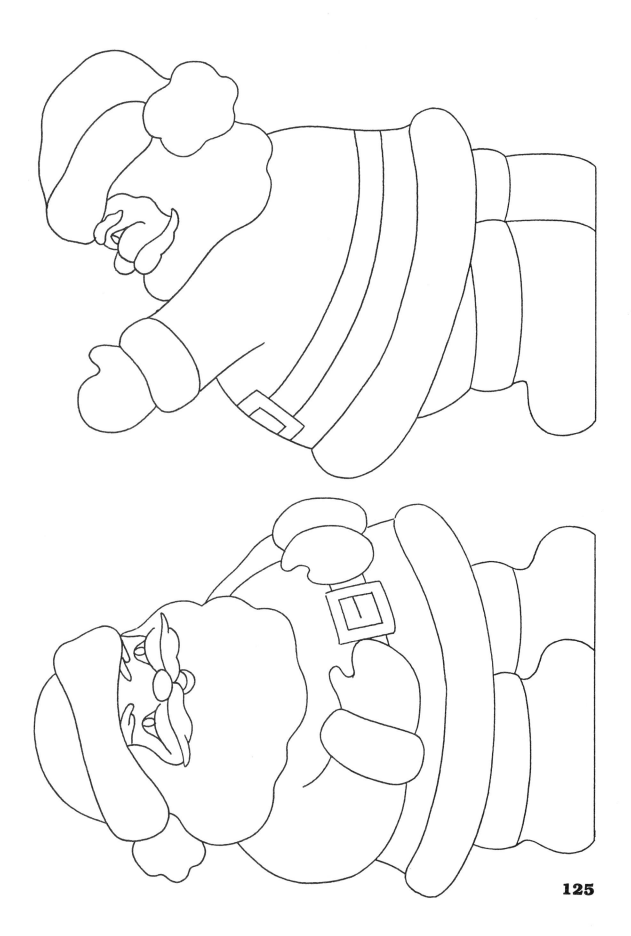

125

A

A

B

A

B

Base, $\frac{1}{4}'' \times 2\frac{1}{4}'' \times 4\frac{1}{2}''$.

*Trees at left, ¾" thick.
Dimensional trees at right
made from ¼"-thick stock.*

*Trees, 1½" thick, and ¾"-thick
angel with plain antique
finish.*

*Wreath, ¾" thick, with ⅜"-
thick bow overlay.*

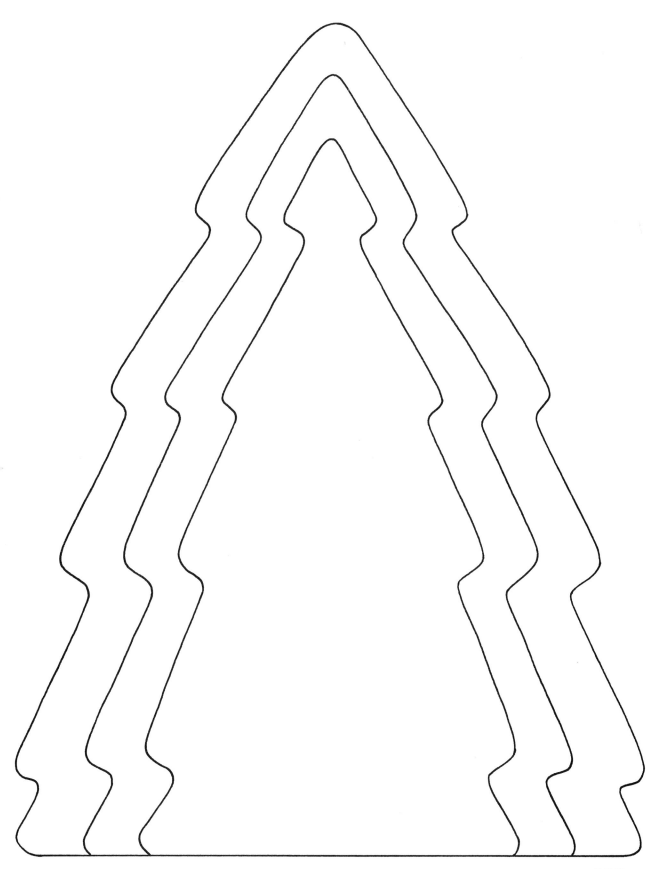

129

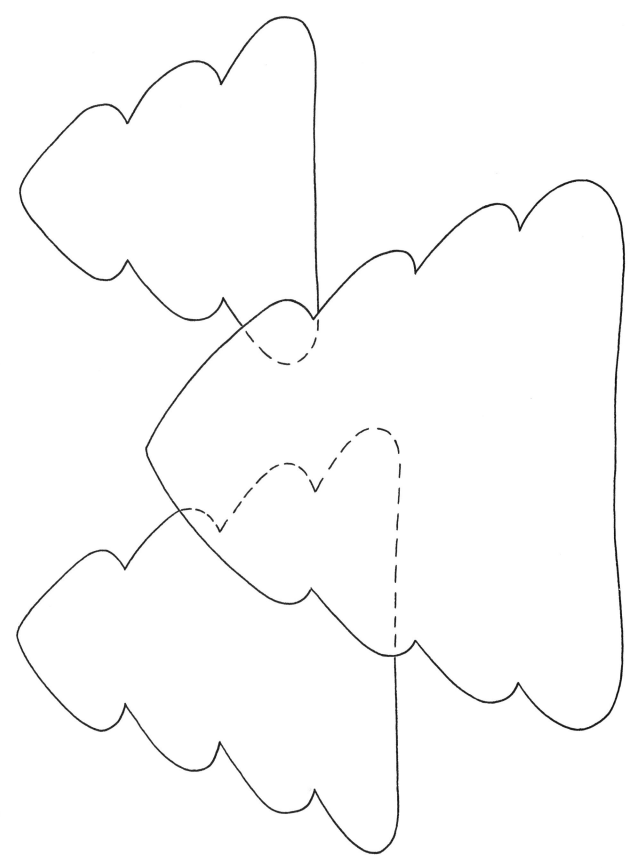

131

Circular dashed line indicates optional back rabbet cut for use as a picture frame.

Rocking horse sawn from ¾"-thick and ½"-thick softwood, painted with darker edges.

133

Trees and horse, ¾″ thick, with antique finish.

135

140

142

Fretwork angel. Cut from any suitable material.

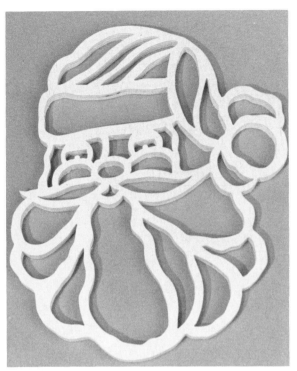

Unfinished plywood, ¼" thick, was used for this cutout.

This plywood cutout can be made from any thickness material and can either be painted or left unfinished.

Plywood, ¼" thick, was used for this cutout.

143

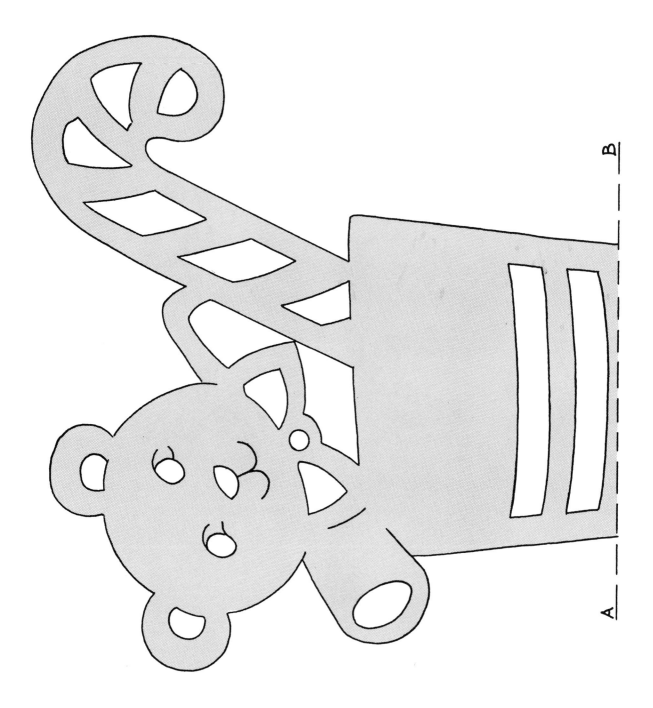

A

B

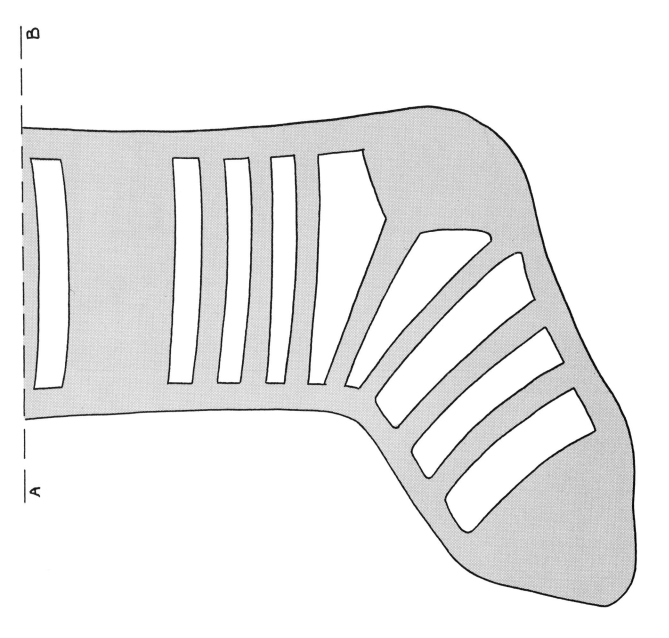

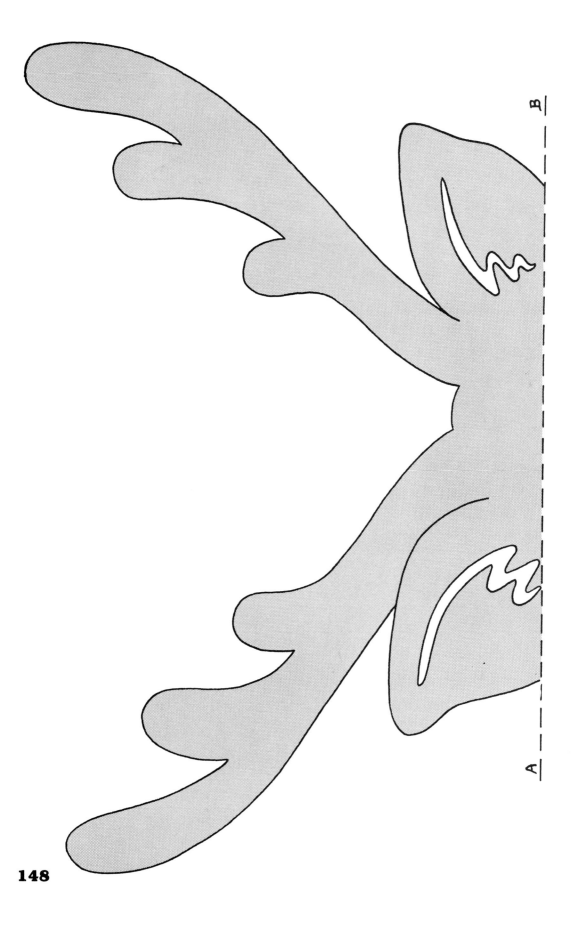

A

B

148

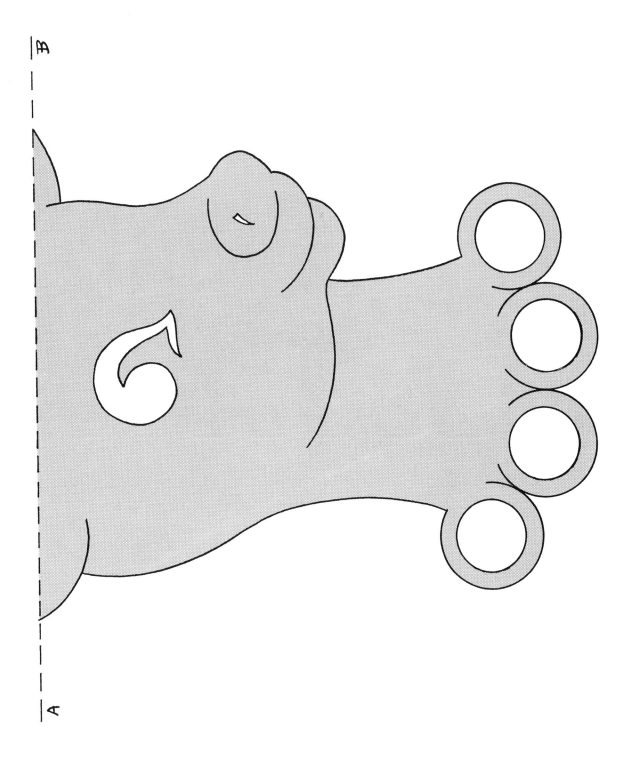

B

A

149

150

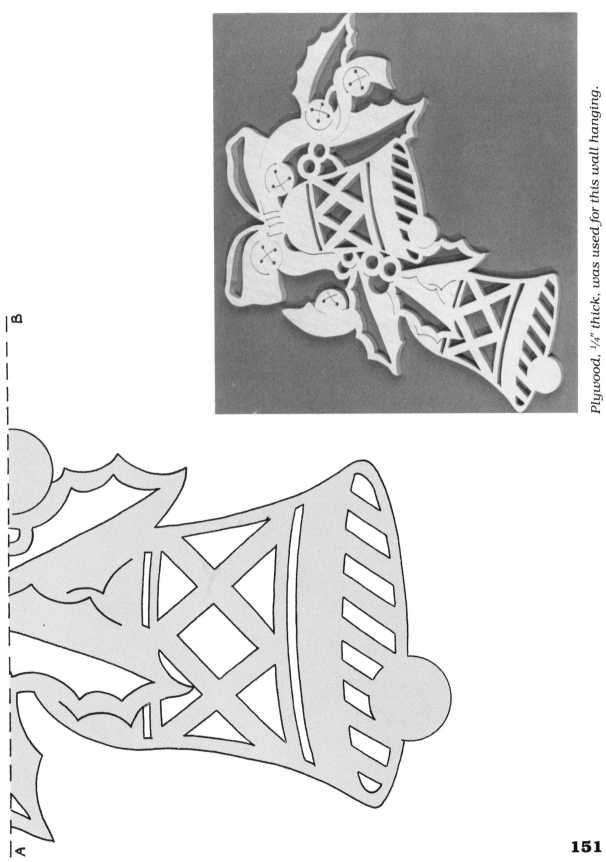

B

A

Plywood, ¹⁄₄″ thick, was used for this wall hanging.

Wall or trivet design. Cut from any available thickness.

152

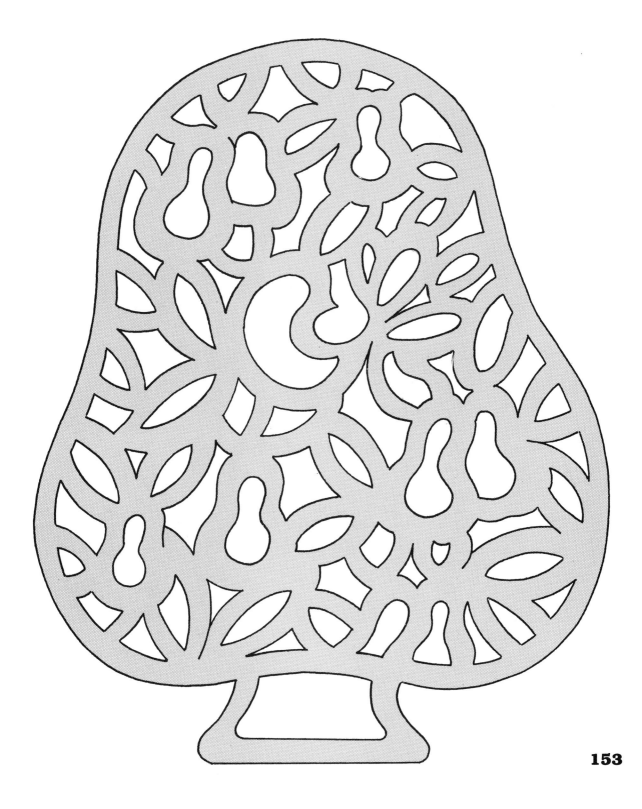

153

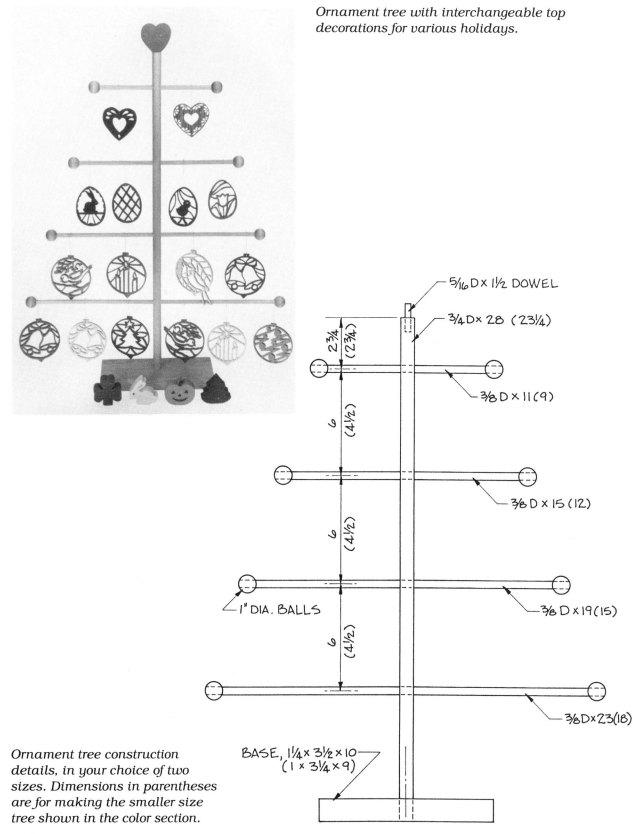

Ornament tree with interchangeable top decorations for various holidays.

5/16 D × 1½ DOWEL

¾ D × 28 (23¼)

2¾ (2¾)

⅜ D × 11 (9)

6 (4½)

⅜ D × 15 (12)

6 (4½)

1" DIA. BALLS

⅜ D × 19 (15)

6 (4½)

⅜ D × 23 (18)

BASE, 1¼ × 3½ × 10
(1 × 3¼ × 9)

Ornament tree construction details, in your choice of two sizes. Dimensions in parentheses are for making the smaller size tree shown in the color section.

154

Patterns for interchangeable top decorations of the ornament tree.

155

Current Books by Patrick Spielman

Alphabets and Designs for Wood Signs. 50 alphabet patterns, plans for many decorative designs, the latest on hand carving, routing, cutouts, and sandblasting. Pricing data. Photo gallery (4 pages in color) of wood signs by professionals from across the U.S. Over 200 illustrations. 128 pages.

Carving Large Birds. Spielman and renowned woodcarver Bill Dehos show how to carve a fascinating array of large birds. All of the tools and basic techniques that are used are discussed in depth, and hundreds of photos, illustrations, and patterns are provided for carving graceful swans, majestic eagles, comical-looking penguins, a variety of owls, and scores of other birds. Oversized. 16 pages in full color. 192 pages.

Carving Wild Animals: Life-Size Wood Figures. Spielman and renowned woodcarver Bill Dehos show how to carve more than 20 magnificent creatures of the North American wild. A cougar, black bear, prairie dog, squirrel, raccoon, and fox are some of the life-size animals included. Step-by-step, photo-filled instructions and multiple-view patterns, plus tips on the use of tools, wood selection, finishing, and polishing help you bring each animal to life. Oversized. Over 300 photos; 16 pages in full color. 240 pages.

Classic Fretwork Scroll Saw Patterns. With over 140 imaginative patterns inspired by and derived from mid to late nineteenth century scroll-saw masters, this new book covers nearly 30 categories of patterns and includes a brief review of scroll-saw

techniques and how to work with patterns. The patterns include ornamental numbers and letters, beautiful birds, signs, wall pockets, silhouettes, a sleigh, jewelry boxes, toy furniture, and more. 192 pages.

Gluing & Clamping. A thorough, up-to-date examination of one of the most critical steps in woodworking. Spielman explores the features of every type of glue—from traditional animal-hide glues to the newest epoxies—the clamps and tools needed, the bonding properties of different wood species, safety tips, and all techniques from edge-to-edge and end-to-end gluing to applying plastic laminates. Also included is a glossary of terms. Over 500 illustrations. 256 pages.

Making Country-Rustic Wood Projects. Hundreds of photos, patterns, and detailed scaled drawings reveal construction methods, woodworking techniques, and Spielman's professional secrets for making indoor and outdoor furniture in the distinctly attractive Country-Rustic style. Covered are all aspects of furniture making from choosing the best wood for the job to texturing smooth boards. Among the dozens of projects are mailboxes, cabinets, shelves, coffee tables, weather vanes, doors, panelling, plant stands and many other durable and economical pieces. 400 illustrations. 4 pages in full color. 164 pages.

Making Wood Decoys. A clear step-by-step approach to the basics of decoy carving. This book is abundantly illustrated with closeup photos for designing, selecting, and obtaining woods; tools; feather detailing; painting; and finishing of decorative and working decoys. Six different professional decoy artists are featured. Photo gallery (4 pages in full color) along with numerous detailed plans for various popular decoys. 160 pages.

Making Wood Signs. Designing, selecting woods and tools, and every process through finishing are clearly covered. Hand-carved, power-carved, routed, and sandblasted processes in small to huge signs are presented. Foolproof guides for professional letters and ornaments. Hundreds of photos (4 pages in full color). Lists sources for supplies and special tooling. 144 pages.

Realistic Decoys. Spielman and master carver Keith Bridenhagen reveal their successful techniques for carving, feather texturing, painting, and finishing wood decoys. Details that you can't find elsewhere—anatomy, attitudes, markings, and the easy step-by-step approach to perfect delicate procedures—make this book invaluable. Includes listings for contests, shows, and sources of tools and supplies. 274 closeup photos. 28 in color. 224 pages.

Router Basics. With over 200 closeup step-by-step photos and drawings, this valuable overview will guide the new owner as well as provide a spark to owners for whom the router isn't the tool they turn to most often. Covers all the basic router styles, along with how-it-works descriptions of all its major features. Includes sections on bits and accessories as well as square-cutting and trimming, case and furniture routing, cutting circles and arcs, template and freehand routing, and using the router with a router table. 128 pages.

Router Handbook. With nearly 600 illustrations of every conceivable bit, attachment, jig, and fixture, plus every possible operation, this definitive guide has revolutionized router applications. It begins with safety and maintenance tips, then forges ahead into all aspects of dovetailing, freehanding, advanced duplication, and more. Details for over 50 projects are included. 224 pages.

Router Jigs & Techniques. A practical encyclopedia of information, covering the latest equipment to use with your router, it describes all the newest of commercial routing machines, along with jigs, bits, and other aids and devices. The book not only provides invaluable tips on how to determine the router and bits best suited to your needs, but tells you how to get the most out of your equipment once it is bought. Over 800 photos and illustrations. 384 pages.

Scroll Saw Basics. This overview features more than 275 illustrations covering basic techniques and accessories. Sections include types of saw, features, selection of blades, safety, and how to use patterns. A half-dozen patterns are included to help the scroll saw user get started. Basic cutting techniques are covered including inside cuts, bevel cuts, stack-sawing, and others. 128 pages.

Scroll Saw Fretwork Patterns. This companion book to *Scroll Saw Fretwork Techniques and Projects* features over 200 fabulous full-size fretwork patterns. These patterns include the most popular classic designs of the past, plus an array of imaginative contemporary ones. Choose from a variety of numbers, signs, brackets, animals, miniatures, and silhouettes, and many more. 256 pages.

Scroll Saw Fretwork Techniques & Projects. This companion book to *Scroll Saw Fretwork Patterns* offers a study in the historical development of fretwork, as well as the tools, techniques, materials, and project styles that have evolved over the past 130 years. Every intricate turn and cut is explained with over 550 step-by-step photos and illustrations. Patterns for all 32 projects are shown in full color. The book also covers some modern scroll-sawing machines and current state-of-the-art fretwork and fine scroll sawing techniques. 232 pages.

Scroll Saw Handbook. This companion volume to *Scroll Saw Pattern Book* covers the essentials of this versatile tool, including the basics (how scroll saws work, blades to use, etc.) and the advantages and disadvantages of the general types and specific brand-name models available on the market. All cutting techniques are detailed, including compound and bevel sawing, making inlays, reliefs, and recesses, cutting metals and other nonwoods, and marquetry. There's even a section on transferring patterns to wood! Over 500 illustrations. 256 pages.

Scroll Saw Pattern Book. This companion book to *Scroll Saw Handbook* contains over 450 workable patterns for making wall plaques, refrigerator magnets, candle holders, pegboards, jewelry, ornaments, shelves, brackets, picture frames, signboards, and many more projects. Beginners and experienced scroll saw users alike will find something to intrigue and challenge them. 256 pages.

Scroll Saw Puzzle Patterns. 80 full-size patterns for jigsaw puzzles, standup puzzles and inlay puzzles. With meticulous attention to detail, Patrick and Patricia Spielman provide instruction and step-by-step photos, along with tips on tools and wood selections, for making standup puzzles in the shape of dinosaurs, camels, hippopotamuses, alligators—even a family of elephants! Inlay puzzle patterns include basic shapes, numbers, an accurate piece-together map of the United States and a

host of other colorful educational and enjoyable games for children. 8 pages of color. 256 pages.

Sharpening Basics. This overview goes well beyond the "basics" to become a major up-to-date reference work featuring more than 300 detailed illustrations (mostly photos) to explain every facet of tool sharpening. Sections include bench sharpening tools, sharpening machines, and safety. Chapters cover cleaning tools and sharpening all sorts of tools including chisels, plane blades (irons), hand knives, carving tools, turning tools, drill and boring tools, router and shaper tools, jointer and planer knives, drivers and scrapers, and, of course, saws. 144 pages.

Spielman's Original Scroll Saw Patterns. 262 full-size patterns that don't appear elsewhere feature teddy bears, dinosaurs, sports figures, dancers, cowboy cutouts, Christmas ornaments, and dozens more. Fretwork patterns are included for a Viking ship, framed cutouts, wall-hangers, key-chain miniatures, jewelry, self-decoration, and much more. Hundreds of step-by-step photos and drawings show how to flop, repeat, and crop each design for thousands of variations. 4 pages of color. 228 pages.

Working Green Wood with PEG. Covers every process for making beautiful, inexpensive projects from green wood without cracking, splitting, or warping. Hundreds of clear photos and drawings show every step from obtaining the raw wood through shaping, treating, and finishing your PEG-treated projects. 175 unusual project ideas. Lists supply sources. 160 pages.

Index